POETRY ADVENTURES

UNDERNEATH MY BED

LIST POEMS

BRIAN P. CLEARY

ILLUSTRATIONS BY
RICHARD WATSON

M MILLBROOK PRESS/MINNEAPOLIS

To Xochitl and Frankie
—B.P.C.

To Jen and Martin
—R.W.

Millbrook Press
A division of Lerner Publishing Group, Inc.
241 First Avenue North
Minneapolis, MN 55401 USA

For reading levels and more information, look up this title at www.lernerbooks.com.

Main body text set in Klepto ITC Std Regular 15/20.
Typeface provided by International Typeface Corp.

Library of Congress Cataloging-in-Publication Data

Names: Cleary, Brian P., 1959– author. | Watson, Richard, 1980– illustrator.
Title: Underneath my bed : list poems / Brian P. Cleary ; [illustrated by Richard Watson].
Description: Minneapolis : Millbrook Press, [2017] | Audience: Age: 7–11. | Audience: Grade: 4 to 6.
Identifiers: LCCN 2015043883 | ISBN 9781467793438 (hardcover : acid-free paper) |
    ISBN 9781512412109 (softcover : acid-free paper) | ISBN 9781512411126 (ebook pdf)
Classification: LCC PS3553.L39144 A6 2017 | DDC 811/.54—dc23

LC record available at http://lccn.loc.gov/2015043883

Manufactured in the United States of America
1-38398-20296-4/8/2016

TABLE OF CONTENTS

What Is a List Poem?. 4

At the Bus Stop. 6
Yellow 7
The Joy of Discovery 8
Great-Grandmother's Pet Store 10
My Brother's Wish List 12
The School Microwave 14
At the Lost and Found 16
Come April. 17
Our Alphabetical Classroom 18
No Wonder. 20
Going Green 22
At Summer Camp. 24
The Glove Compartment of Our Van. 26
My Teacher's Ties 28
In the Pockets of My Cargo Shorts. 30

Further Reading 32

WHaT Is a LiST PoeM?

Just like the name suggests, these poems list
things,
places,
people,
sounds,
emotions,
colors,
events,
and more.

They can range in tone from serious to silly, and they
may or may not rhyme. They might make you
think,
smile,
squirm,
nod your head,
giggle,
wince,
or
sigh.

Here's a look at one. Do you see how the poem has a list-like quality to it?

ON BROWN ROAD

Mrs. Darden loves her garden.
Ms. Matousek teaches music.
Mr. Gattan speaks pig latin.
Mrs. Triechel owns a cycle.
Dr. Taylor was a sailor.
Mrs. Durken's always workin'.
Miss Garcia drives a Kia.
Mr. Austin moved from Boston.
Miss McDuggle likes to juggle.
Mrs. Manak's a mechanic.
Mr. Pride cooks outside.
Mrs. Miles always smiles.

So, ask yourself: What are a bunch of things your cat does? If you made the shopping list at your house, what might be on it? What places would you like to visit? All of these can be the beginning of a list and, therefore, a list poem. Now, don't make a list of excuses—get busy writing!

AT THE BUS STOP

Jennifer jumps rope.

Tonya texts.

Tony twirls like a ballerina.

Hailey hums.

William whistles.

Chloe catches up on reading.

Luke listens to tunes.

Miles munches.

Peyton plays I spy.

Jackson jokes.

Logan laughs.

Shawn shows Cheyenne the green, scaly, slimy bug he found in his bed this morning.

Yellow

Butterscotch and bumblebees,
ears of corn and mac and cheese,
pet canaries, dandelions,
those silly shoes of Uncle Brian's,
scrambled eggs and globs of mustard,
caution signs, banana custard,
smiley faces, butterflies,
rubber chickens, lemon pies,
an ancient book that you might read,
the snow right where a dog just peed,
a daffodil, the stars and sun—
oops, my cab's here—gotta run!

THE JOY OF DISCOVERY

Each week, I'm asked to clean my room, but what I do instead
is simply take the whole week's mess to stash beneath my bed.
Then came the day I didn't have a single thing to wear
or read or dry myself with, so I took a look down there.
I found two books, three towels, some long-thought-lost remotes,
cereal and sunscreen and two fall-and-winter coats,
pizza crust, some pants and shirts, some shorts and underpants,
socks and shoes, a sticky, swirly sucker, . . . and some ants.

GREAT-GRANDMOTHER'S PET STORE

Great-Grandmother ran a popular shop, according to Grandma and Daddy. Customers came from all over the state to her pet store in west Cincinnati.

She had chickens, Chihuahuas, chinchillas, and chipmunks,
greyhounds and geckos and geese,
pelicans, poodles and panthers . . . plus parrots
(which sold for a dollar apiece!).

Kangaroos, kittens, koalas, and kiwis
would play on the shop's second floor.
It's always such fun to hear Grandma and Daddy
tell tales of Great-Grandmother's store.

MY BROTHER'S WISH LIST

An eight-pound box of gummy bears
and one electric scooter,
X-ray vision goggles and
a wristwatch-sized computer,
a four-foot-high aquarium,
with twelve fluorescent guppies,
a living, breathing dinosaur
and four robotic puppies,
a trampoline-sized pizza
(with both cheese and pepperoni),
a room that's made of Legos
and one polka-dotted pony,
Jet Skis and a jetpack,
plus a trip to France or Greece,
a kitten that does math homework,
oh yeah . . . and world peace.

WORLD PEACE!

THE SCHOOL MICROWAVE

The microwave at school is gross;
it has the caked remains
of stuff that looks a bit like blood
and scabs and parts of brains.

You see the crumbs from fish sticks
and the sauce from fettuccine.
The noodle types found there include
spaghetti and linguine.

Nachos? Cocoa? Tenders?
You'll find signs of each of these
along with chicken patties, eggs,
and several kinds of cheese.

With hardened broth and hot dog juice,
the sides are brown and rough.
But whatever I heat up in there
tastes like my favorite stuff!

15

AT THE LOST AND FOUND

I go check out the lost and found
each week or so at school.
I've gotten books and thermoses
and other stuff that's cool.
Games and high-tech gadgets,
a lanyard for my key.
It's sort of like a store at school
where everything is free.

COME APRIL

Come April,
windows open,
baseballs fly,
birds cheep,
bunnies hop,
rain falls,
and crocuses sing to the heavens.

OUR ALPHABETICAL CLASSROOM

Alison's a chatterbox. Ben is always crying.
Chloe smells like chicken soup, and Dylan's often lying.
Ethan holds his breath sometimes until his face is florid.
Fiona drew another set of eyebrows on her for'ead.

Gracie is the teacher's pet. Henry clicks his braces.
Izzy's chair is always damp whenever we switch places.
Jude is late most every day, and Kylie loves the drama.
Logan can't be more than twenty paces from his mama.

Me? I spill most everything, and Nicholas is pushy.
Oscar taped a Kick Me sign on his own little tushy.
Pat and Quinn both interrupt, and Riley likes to tell.
Sophie's always bossing us, and Taylor is as well.

Ursula cannot recall a thing that she's been taught.
Vicki hums a little tune whenever deep in thought.
Wyatt's always bragging that he has eleven toes;
he makes a little whistling sound when breathing out his nose.

Xavier taps the gerbil cage and just ignores the teacher.
Yosef does it too and even climbed in with the creature.
Zoe has a made-up friend to chat with, text, and call.
Although our class sounds sort of strange, I kind of like them all!

NO WONDER

Stegosauruses
had no skateboards,
no electronic tablets,
no Coca-Cola,
no gaming consoles,
no bubble gum,
no TV,
no Internet,
no pizza,
no basketballs,
no ice cream,
no smartphones,
no bicycles,
no french fries,
no amusement parks,
and
no Oreos,
. . . and we wonder why they didn't stick around.

GOING GREEN

I've been dripping like a faucet from my nose for days and days—
ever since the day my allergies kicked in.
My phone is kind of sticky, and my doughnut has a glaze.
There's goop upon my shirt and violin.

I've got it on my locker, in my pencil case and books.
On my jacket, there's a green and shiny spot.
It's dotted both my socks and shoes—I get some crazy looks.
Don't tell me that it's funny . . . 'cause it's snot!

AT SUMMER CAMP

Beestings and mosquito bites,
centipedes and lice and mites,
heat and sunburn, ancient rafts,
making lots of useless crafts,
slugs and bugs and spiders creeping,
homesick bunkmate's nightly weeping,
waking up to shrieking whistles,
getting pricked among the thistles,
heavy backpacks, soggy shoes,
tiny cuts that itch and ooze,
corny songs and no TVs,
hives of hornets, wasps, and bees.
Camp can surely be a bummer;
can't wait till I come back next summer!

The Glove Compartment of Our Van

The glove compartment of our van
has napkins, gum, and maps,
sunglasses, a first aid kit,
a pair of baseball caps,
old receipts and paperwork,
a flashlight and some mints,
a tiny thing of mouthwash
if somebody wants to rinse,
ketchup packets, tissues,
a lint brush and some wipes,
coupons, pen, a notepad
that has blue-and-yellow stripes.
The glove compartment of our van
has snacks my mother loves.
The one thing you won't find in there?
A single pair of gloves.

MY Teacher's Ties

My teacher wears a different tie
for each day all year through.
One has baseballs, one has anchors,
one, a kangaroo.

Some are skinny, some are wide,
a couple, frayed and torn.
He never wears the same one twice—
I've tracked each one he's worn.

There's every kind of color,
green and orange and pink and navy.
One has little flecks of brown
(I'm hoping that it's gravy).

Some tie up in great big bows,
and some are polka-dotted.
One still had the price tag
from the men's store where he got it.

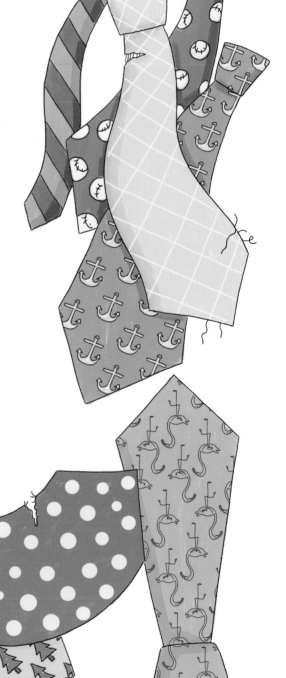

He's famous for his splashy prints—
like parrots and flamingos,
doggies, like dalmatians,
also dinosaurs and dingoes.

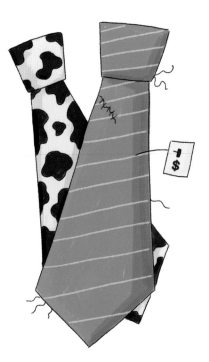

Christmas ties? Thanksgiving ties?
Halloween? For sure!
He's got one just for Groundhog Day
and one for Yom Kippur.

Some kids think it's kind of strange,
but I'm not one to scoff;
I figure that they help to keep
his head from falling off.

IN THE POCKETS OF MY CARGO SHORTS

A photo of my schnauzer, Dave, and one of Richard Nixon,
a cell phone from eight years ago that needs a little fixin',
half a double cheeseburger, half a pint of soup,
a soggy, old toupee I found that smells a bit like poop.
A deck of cards, eleven cents, a salamander, dice,
seashells, a harmonica that's old but pretty nice.
Shoehorn, bike horn, French horn, and a yo-yo (minus string).
What's inside my pockets? Well, you might say everything!

FURTHER READING

BOOKS

Heard, Georgia, ed. *Falling Down the Page: A Book of List Poems*. New York: Roaring Brook Press, 2009.
This anthology showcases list poems that all have to do with experiences kids have throughout the school year.

Janeczko, Paul B., ed. *A Kick in the Head: An Everyday Guide to Poetic Forms*. Cambridge, MA: Candlewick, 2005.
This collection of poems showcases many different forms, including the sonnet, pantoum, elegy, and couplet.

Prelutsky, Jack. *Pizza, Pigs, and Poetry: How to Write a Poem*. New York: Greenwillow Books, 2008.
Would you like to write your own poetry? Here are some expert tips for turning your own experiences and stories about your family, your pets, and your friends into poems.

WEBSITES

Giggle Poetry: How to Write a "What Bugs Me" List Poem
http://www.gigglepoetry.com/poetryclassdetail.aspx?LessonPlanID=17
Bruce Lansky explains how list poems work and offers suggestions for how to get started writing your own list poem.

Poems Kids Like
https://www.poets.org/poetsorg/text/poems-kids
This site provides links to poems that are popular with kids, including the list poems "At the Zoo," "Bleezer's Ice Cream," "Mother Doesn't Want a Dog," "Nonsense Alphabet," and "Sick."

Poetry for Kids: How to Write a Funny List Poem
http://www.poetry4kids.com/blog/lessons/how-to-write-a-funny-list-poem/
Find more tips about writing list poems from Kenn Nesbitt as well as links to additional examples.